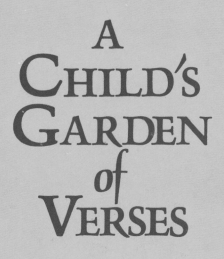

A CHILD'S GARDEN of VERSES

This 1986 edition published by Derrydale Books,
distributed by Crown Publishers, Inc., 225
Park Avenue South, New York, New York 10003
Printed in Italy
h g f e d c b a

ISBN 0-517-62646-2

A CHILD'S GARDEN of VERSES

Abridged Edition

Robert Louis Stevenson
Illustrated by Jessie Willcox Smith

Derrydale Books
New York

BED IN SUMMER

IN winter I get up at night
And dress by yellow candle-light.
In summer, quite the other way,
I have to go to bed by day.

I have to go to bed and see
The birds still hopping on the tree,
Or hear the grown-up people's feet
Still going past me in the street.

And does it not seem hard to you,
When all the sky is clear and blue,
And I should like so much to play,
To have to go to bed by day?

JESSIE WILLCOX SMITH.

TIME TO RISE

A BIRDIE with a yellow bill
    Hopped upon the window sill,
    Cocked his shining eye and said:
    "Ain't you 'shamed, you sleepy-head!"

WHOLE DUTY OF CHILDREN

A CHILD should always say what's true
    And speak when he is spoken to,
    And behave mannerly at table;
    At least as far as he is able.

MARCHING SONG

BRING the comb and play upon it!
    Marching, here we come!
    Willie cocks his highland bonnet,
Johnnie beats the drum.

Mary Jane commands the party,
    Peter leads the rear;
Feet in time, alert and hearty,
    Each a Grenadier!

All in the most martial manner
    Marching double-quick;
While the napkin, like a banner,
    Waves upon the stick!

Here's enough of fame and pillage,
    Great commander Jane!
Now that we've been round the village,
    Let's go home again.

WHERE GO THE BOATS?

DARK brown is the river,
　　Golden is the sand.
　　It flows along for ever,
With trees on either hand.

Green leaves a-floating,
　　Castles of the foam,
Boats of mine a-boating —
　　Where will all come home?

On goes the river
　　And out past the mill,
Away down the valley,
　　Away down the hill.

Away down the river,
　　A hundred miles or more,
Other little children
　　Shall bring my boats ashore.

FROM A RAILWAY CARRIAGE

FASTER than fairies, faster than witches,
    Bridges and houses, hedges and ditches;
    And charging along like troops in a battle
All through the meadows the horses and cattle:
All of the sights of the hill and the plain
Fly as thick as driving rain;
And ever again, in the wink of an eye,
Painted stations whistle by.

Here is a child who clambers and scrambles,
All by himself and gathering brambles;
Here is a tramp who stands and gazes;
And there is the green for stringing the daisies
Here is a cart run away in the road
Lumping along with man and load;
And here is a mill, and there is a river:
Each a glimpse and gone for ever!

FOREIGN LANDS

UP into the cherry tree
    Who should climb but little me?
    I held the trunk with both my hands
    And looked abroad on foreign lands.

I saw the next door garden lie,
Adorned with flowers, before my eye,
And many pleasant places more
That I had never seen before.

I saw the dimpling river pass
And be the sky's blue looking-glass;
The dusty roads go up and down
With people tramping in to town.

If I could find a higher tree
Farther and farther I should see,
To where the grown-up river slips
Into the sea among the ships,

To where the roads on either hand
Lead onward into fairy land,
Where all the children dine at five,
And all the playthings come alive.

THE FLOWERS

ALL the names I know from nurse:
Gardener's garters, Shepherd's purse,
Bachelor's buttons, Lady's smock,
And the Lady Hollyhock.

Fairy places, fairy things,
Fairy woods where the wild bee wings,
Tiny trees for tiny dames —
These must all be fairy names!

Tiny woods below whose boughs
Shady fairies weave a house;
Tiny tree-tops, rose or thyme,
Where the braver fairies climb!

Fair are grown-up people's trees,
But the fairest woods are these;
Where, if I were not so tall,
I should live for good and all.

THE HAYLOFT

THROUGH all the pleasant meadow-side
   The grass grew shoulder-high,
   Till the shining scythes went far and wide
And cut it down to dry.

Those green and sweetly smelling crops
   They led in waggons home;
And they piled them here in mountain tops
   For mountaineers to roam.

Here is Mount Clear, Mount Rusty-Nail,
   Mount Eagle and Mount High; —
The mice that in these mountains dwell,
   No happier are than I!

Oh, what a joy to clamber there,
   Oh, what a place for play,
With the sweet, the dim, the dusty air,
   The happy hills of hay!

MY SHADOW

I HAVE a little shadow that goes in and out with me,
　　And what can be the use of him is more than I can
　　　　see.
He is very, very like me from the heels up to the head;
And I see him jump before me, when I jump into my bed.

The funniest thing about him is the way he likes to grow —
Not at all like proper children, which is always very slow;
For he sometimes shoots up taller like an india-rubber ball,
And he sometimes gets so little that there's none of him at all.

He hasn't got a notion of how children ought to play,
And can only make a fool of me in every sort of way.

He stays so close beside me, he's a coward you can see;
I'd think shame to stick to nursie as that shadow sticks to
　　me!

One morning, very early, before the sun was up,
I rose and found the shining dew on every buttercup;
But my lazy little shadow, like an arrant sleepy-head,
Had stayed at home behind me and was fast asleep in bed.

RAIN

THE rain is raining all around,
  It falls on field and tree,
It rains on the umbrellas here,
  And on the ships at sea.

AT THE SEA-SIDE

WHEN I was down beside the sea
  A wooden spade they gave to me
  To dig the sandy shore.

My holes were empty like a cup.
In every hole the sea came up,
  Till it could come no more.

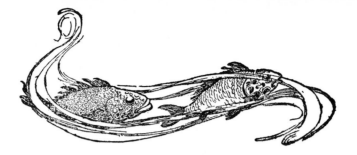

LOOKING–GLASS RIVER

SMOOTH it glides upon its travel,
Here a wimple, there a gleam —
O the clean gravel!
O the smooth stream!

Sailing blossoms, silver fishes,
Paven pools as clear as air —
How a child wishes
To live down there!

We can see our coloured faces
Floating on the shaken pool
Down in cool places,
Dim and very cool;

Till a wind or water wrinkle,
Dipping marten, plumping trout,
Spreads in a twinkle
And blots all out.

See the rings pursue each other;
All below grows black as night,
Just as if mother
Had blown out the light!

Patience, children, just a minute —
See the spreading circles die;
The stream and all in it
Will clear by-and-by.

PIRATE STORY

THREE of us afloat in the meadow by the swing,
   Three of us aboard in the basket on the lea.
Winds are in the air, they are blowing in the spring,
   And waves are on the meadow like the waves there
      are at sea.

Where shall we adventure, to-day that we're afloat,
   Wary of the weather and steering by a star?
Shall it be to Africa, a-steering of the boat,
   To Providence, or Babylon, or off to Malabar?

Hi! but here's a squadron a-rowing on the sea —
   Cattle on the meadow a-charging with a roar!
Quick, and we'll escape them, they're as mad as they can be,
   The wicket is the harbour and the garden is the shore.

THE SWING

HOW do you like to go up in a swing,
  Up in the air so blue?
  Oh, I do think it the pleasantest thing
Ever a child can do!

Up in the air and over the wall,
  Till I can see so wide,
Rivers and trees and cattle and all
  Over the countryside —

Till I look down on the garden green,
  Down on the roof so brown —
Up in the air I go flying again,
  Up in the air and down!

PICTURE–BOOKS IN WINTER

SUMMER fading, winter comes —
    Frosty mornings, tingling thumbs,
    Window robins, winter rooks,
    And the picture story-books.

Water now is turned to stone
Nurse and I can walk upon;
Still we find the flowing brooks
In the picture story-books.

All the pretty things put by,
Wait upon the children's eye,
Sheep and shepherds, trees and crooks,
In the picture story-books.

We may see how all things are,
Seas and cities, near and far,
And the flying fairies' looks,
In the picture story-books.

How am I to sing your praise,
Happy chimney-corner days,
Sitting safe in nursery nooks,
Reading picture story-books?

NORTH–WEST PASSAGE

WHEN the bright lamp is carried in,
The sunless hours again begin ;
O'er all without, in field and lane,
The haunted night returns again.

Now we behold the embers flee
About the firelit hearth ; and see
Our faces painted as we pass,
Like pictures, on the window-glass.

Must we to bed indeed? Well then,
Let us arise and go like men,
And face with an undaunted tread
The long black passage up to bed.

Farewell, O brother, sister, sire !
O pleasant party round the fire !
The songs you sing, the tales you tell,
Till far to-morrow, fare ye well !

THE LAND OF COUNTERPANE

WHEN I was sick and lay a-bed,
I had two pillows at my head,
And all my toys beside me lay
To keep me happy all the day.

And sometimes for an hour or so
I watched my leaden soldiers go,
With different uniforms and drills,
Among the bed-clothes, through the hills;

And sometimes sent my ships in fleets
All up and down among the sheets;
Or brought my trees and houses out,
And planted cities all about.

I was the giant great and still
That sits upon the pillow-hill,
And sees before him, dale and plain,
The pleasant land of counterpane.

TO ANY READER

AS from the house your mother sees
You playing round the garden trees,
So you may see, if you will look
Through the windows of this book,
Another child, far, far away,
And in another garden, play.
But do not think you can at all,
By knocking on the window, call
That child to hear you. He intent
Is all on his play-business bent.

He does not hear; he will not look,
Nor yet be lured out of this book.
For, long ago, the truth to say,
He has grown up and gone away,
And it is but a child of air
That lingers in the garden there.